A JOURNEY THROUGH GENERATIONS

Biography of an immigrant from India in USA

Andreos

ISBN: 1-4033-3048-4 (Electronic)
ISBN: 1-4033-3049-2 (Softcover)

Library of Congress Control Number:
2002105739

This book is printed on acid free paper.

Printed in the United States of America
Bloomington, IN

1stBooks - rev. 07/16/02

INTRODUCTION

This book is a biography of a person who grew up in India and then migrated to USA at the age of 25. The author narrates his life in simple language and provides a good picture of the social and cultural surroundings that influenced him. Most of the professionally qualified immigrants from India in the seventies had similar experiences. The intention of the author is to provide an opportunity to the readers a perspective of one of those immigrants from India to USA.

This book tries to reason with the circumstances one is born and bought up. It analyses the influence of culture and social traditions on the life of an individual. It explores the effects of the time and place on one's life. It relates the experiences of each generation and the significance of history. The author tries to look at all these factors in relation to his life. He looks at his life through generations.

Finally, the author tries to find an answer to the question, what is the ultimate goal of life? The author tries to reason with the teachings of religion. He finds that too many questions are unanswered. He is not confused about life in this world, but doubts about a life after death. He believes that the religions preach life after death to their followers as means of hope and faith.

The author wishes that the readers of this book will be able to analyze their life look back in history and find a goal for life. The author would like every individual who reads this book can enjoy rest of the life with optimism and sense of purpose. The author says, "We must make the world a better place to live by our deeds".

Chapter I

My village and family.

Growing up in a village bordering a small town in the State of Kerala, India did not have any influence on my personality. I tried to develop a personality of my own even though I was influenced by the events around me. Life is full of experiences. A person like me, grew up in a village in an underdeveloped third world country, received the privileges that most of the people could not get, completed graduate education, migrated to USA in the early seventies and developed a good professional career has lot to write about. My first twenty-five years was mostly spent with my parents, brothers and sister in the village called

1

Kollad bordering a small town called Kottayam. My father was a retired army civilian officer, who worked in the British army from 1941-51. Our home was built in 1948, the year I was born. My father came back and settled in the village with his wife and four children. I have an older sister and two older brothers. A brother was born to me in 1951. My father started some commodity business initially and lost all his savings. Then he started working as a sales manager in an auto parts store. My father has acquired some farming property. Therefore we had some income from the farm products and were able to get vegetables, rice etc. from our own farm. My mother was not a very responsible person. We always had servants in the house to help my mother to cook, clean and perform other work including laundry, yard cleaning etc. Cooking was done by wood burning stove. Water is collected from the well by pulling in small buckets connected through a pulley. Clothes were washed by hitting on flat rock stones and dried hanging on the rope. We used to eat four meals, breakfast, lunch, evening snacks and dinner. Main dish for lunch and dinner was rice and most of the time breakfast also was rice. There were other products like tapioca, banana, jackfruit, mango etc. from the farm used for cooking various dishes.

Our village had three primary schools, two owned by Christian churches and one by government. There was no high school in our village. A middle school was started by a Christian minister, which my sister and I attended. My eldest brother attended a high school in the next village and he was the only person graduated with distinction from that school. My other brothers and I attended a Christian high school in town and my sister attended a catholic girl's high school in town. We all graduated high school with distinction. We all attended colleges. My older brothers and sister took Bachelor degrees and my younger brother and I took Master degrees.

Everybody knew each other in the village. Most of the people were either Hindus or Christians. There were no Muslims in our village. There were so called scheduled caste called Pulayans, Parayans and Ulladans. They were mostly Christians in our village. Then there were some trade caste people, Mara Asari (carpenters), Kalle Asai (masons), Kollans (iron smith), Thattans (gold smith), Paravans (tree climbers), Velans (painters) and Kaniyans (astrologers), who were all considered low caste Hindus. Most of the Hindus in our village belonged to a caste called Ezhavas and they were considered lower caste Hindus below Brahmins and Nairs. Ezhavas belong to an organization called Sree Narayana Dharma Paripalana Sangham (SNDP) formed by Sree Narayana Guru, a very revered reformer. Most of the Christians were called Syrian Christians because they considered themselves ancestors of the original Christians converted by St. Thomas, disciple of Jesus who was believed to have visited our State in A.D 52. There were different church denominations, Catholic, Eastern Orthodox, Anglican, Seventh day Adventists, Pentecostal etc. The Syrian Christians think that they are upper class, since they claim to have been converted from a Brahmin caste called Nampoodhiris. Both my parents belong to Syrian Christian families.

My father was a very active, fun loving, liberal minded person, My father had two brothers and three sisters. Both his brothers were schoolteachers. My mother was a cool personality. My mother had three sisters and seven brothers. I haven't seen my father's parents and have seen a picture of my grand mother. I have heard that my grand father was a nice person and he lost most of his property by putting up as collateral for a cousin's loan. I do not remember seeing my mother's father. He worked as a forest officer. His father was an Anglican minister and an eye doctor. My mother's mother managed to bring up eleven children. My mother grew up in a village about sixteen miles from where we lived. Transportation was not that easy those days and for most people even a bus ride was not affordable. We had to walk two miles and then take a bus to reach mother's house. We used to visit our mother's house during summer vacation, months of April and May. Many of our cousins would be there. My grandmother used to line us up and make us sit on the floor and serve food. A record player was there at my mother's house, which my uncle played every evening.

Life as a child was very exciting. We had to help our father in the farm. There were farm workers. During the rice harvest time, we all had to help. My sister did not have to do any outside work. Only help my mother in cooking or cleaning. Most of the vegetables grew in our farm. Pepper from which black pepper is produced was an income producing cultivation. Similarly excess rice, coconuts, banana etc. were sold to retail merchants for income. During the harvest season availability of food was in plenty.

Most of the villagers were poor. They had no land of their own and lived in somebody else's land or illegally in government owned property. Many of them could not afford three meals a day, sometimes even a meal. My mother used to give away food to our poor neighbors even if sometimes we did not have enough. Because of her good nature many people took advantage of her. She never got involved in local gossip and was not a jealous person. She often read the book and found happiness in solitude. We had to deal with people who work in the field to fertilize the coconut trees, pepper, banana tree, paddy etc. Paravan, a person belong to a particular caste, used to come once a month to cut down coconuts from the tree and we had to pick them up and collect at one spot. For every three trees he climbed, he used to take one coconut, which was his fee. There was no cash payment. Even in paddy field, during harvest, workers were paid a certain quantity of raw rice for the amount of work they did. The lead worker used to get a higher quantity. Daily wages were not very high and often it included breakfast and lunch at our house. Workers were not allowed to sit with us and they were asked to sit in the kitchen floor and food was served either in pot made of soil or in big banana leaves. They were never allowed to come inside the house unless they have to do some work. There was special storage space for rice in the attic. Mango was pickled in big jars. During the monsoon season, months of June-July, because of continuous rain there will be no farming and therefore workers will have no income. There were one or two cows and several chickens in the farm, which provided us daily milk and eggs. For most of the people this was a luxury. When we enter the house from outside after work, we had to wash our feet. Inside the house, the floors are cement and often dirty.

The standard of living was low. Nobody had a refrigerator. Only one or two persons own a car, few two wheelers and some bicycles. My father had a bicycle, which often was borrowed by his friends. Electric power connection came to our village in 1955, which is very early compared to the rest of the country. Very few people could afford power connection. Most were still using kerosene lamps. Flashlights were not at all affordable to most people. Telephone lines came to our village in the sixties and only a handful of people had telephone connection. There was a post office, which opened only for a few hours.

Only cotton clothes were available in those days. After washing and drying, we had to press them hard with iron heated by burning coconut shells. Each of us had two or three sets of clothes. Poor people could not even afford a full set of clothes. Village men wore mundu (one-piece wrap around) and walked around with bare chest. Poor women wore mundu and blouse (a half top). Older women often did not wear a blouse; some used to cover their chest with a piece of cloth. Under wear or under panties were not at all common. Narrow long piece of cloth tied to the waist called Chela was wrapped under to cover the front and back with a long tail. The only cloth the farm workers wore was Chela when they worked, since they did not want to dirty the one and only Mundu, the wrap around one piece clothe.

Chapter II
India, Its Culture and Traditions

India became independent in 1947. In 1956 then Prime Minister Pandit Jawarlal Nehru redrew the country and formed states based on the language people speak. The state of Kerala was formed for people who speak the language Malayalam, which is my mother tongue. Before it was Travancore-Cochin, the state formed at the time of independence combining the kingdoms of Travancore and Cochin. In fact one of my father's brothers was teaching in the State of Cochin and he had to cross the border before independence. India is a vast country with lot of people. There are fourteen different languages and more than three hundred dialects. Customs and traditions change from place to place even though the basic culture is rooted in Hinduism. There were four major castes among Hindus; Bhramins, Kshathryas, Vysias and Shootras. In different part of India each caste had a different name. Most of them can be identified with their last names. There were lots of tribe communities who mainly live in rural and hilly areas. Many of them had never seen civilization. In the State of Kerala, there are several hill tribes called Malayarayans, Theyans etc. If you travel through India, you will notice the difference in the way they wear the clothes; they build and decorate their houses and the type of food they cook. It is amazing. Hinduism itself is a fascinating religion. Each of these hundreds of different castes, sub castes, and tribes at different regions practice the Hindu religion in a different manner. There are different Gods with different names. Each had a unique culture and followed special traditions. Since, India was ruled by the Moghul kings for more than 400 years, there is a large Muslim population. But, the Muslims in Kerala were different from Muslims from other parts of India. Kerala always had communal harmony.

Social customs were very strange in Kerala also. Caste system in Hindu religion was still prevalent. I have heard from my parents that when Namboodhiris (high cast Hindus) walk, everybody has to move away because they were considered untouchables.

People belong to the lower caste could never socialize with the so-called upper class. Often when upper caste people sit on a chair or bench, the lower caste people sat on the floor. The lower caste people always talked to the upper class using special words of respect. It was unbelievable and amazing. I had problem accepting these traditions, but I had no choice.

Women did not have much freedom outside their homes. Very few women completed high school education and college during my mother's times. My grandmother's period women hardly went to school. During my times women were equally educated like men. Things started to change. But still after school or work, women were supposed to go home straight. They could not hang out. Men could do anything and are not questioned. During my grand mother's times women's job was to bear child and there was no family planning. No contraceptive was available. Most of the families had five to twelve children. Proposed marriages are being practiced even now. During my grand mother's time child marriage was prevalent. Men and women used to get married at the age of 10 to 15. They used to live with the husband's parents and eventually would find out the purpose of marriage and start living as husband and wife. Things started changing during my mother's generation. Still the parents used to fix the marriage. The boy and the girl did not have too much of a say. Now at least the boy and the girl have to like each other.

Women in Kerala did not wear sari. They wore a three piece set; a wrap around (mundu), a blouse and a piece of cloth to cover the chest (kavuni). This dress is still worn by older women. Christian women wear all three pieces in white and they make a special tail in the back by using one end of the wrap. Poor people could not afford full clothing. They often walked around half-naked. My sister had no freedom even when she was attending the college. She had to stay home after school and was not allowed to go out alone. One of us had to always accompany her.

Some of the traditions were funny. Each caste and religion had its own practices and traditions. Even within each religion, different sects had their own customs and practices. Traditions and practices change from region to region. In olden times, when visitors leave your house, you had to accompany them until you see water, a pool, stream or river. Visitors would never say good bye, they could only say that they would return. When a person leaves the house for some important matter, it was believed that the first person facing that person must have good luck. Fire is a symbol of good luck. Therefore, often before leaving the house for some special purpose, wedding etc. someone will cross your path with a lighted lamp. Some of these traditions are still followed.

Respecting the elderly is still an well-accepted tradition. An elderly person always gets preferences and will be seated first wherever they go. They are always offered assistance and younger people never misbehave or talk disrespectfully in front of them. In olden times the grand father or the father had a special chair/resting place in the house, which nobody else can use. In those days a person is considered old at the age of fifty. Life expectancy was 55-65 during the nineteen fifties.

The students as well as the community respected teachers. The teacher, who teaches how to read and write is respected by the student throughout his/her life and often mentioned as the GURU. At all auspicious occasion, like wedding the GURU will be asked to bless the person and was offered a gift. In olden times before actual schools were built home schooling was practiced. The teacher used to visit each home and teach how to read and write.

All were expected to follow the social customs and traditions and those who do not practice were considered out casts. I had problem understanding and following many of those old traditions. Nobody could give any explanation of the need for practicing those customs. Your grand parents and parents followed it and therefore you also follow them. Past practices were always right. Society did not like changes. Some of those practices are hundreds of years old. Many of those traditions were originated from the Hindu religion. Most of the Hindu religious traditions are still being followed.

Like the Dracula stories in the Eastern Europe, there were lot of ghost stories. People believed those stories. For some reason all these ghosts only appear at night when people are sleeping., since they do not like day light. There were no actual eyewitnesses. Story is always that somebody else has seen it. Most of these ghosts supposed to travel from one Hindu temple to another Hindu temple at night. If you are on its path, it will kill you. Similarly, there are YEKSHI stories. Yekshi, a ghost that drinks human blood that appears in front of you at night as a beautiful lady crying for help. When you try to help her, she turns into a devil, kills you and drinks your blood. Devil worship is very common even now. If you want to do some harm to somebody, these devil worshippers will do KOODOTHRAM (Voodoo).

The huge cultural difference between people of India from different regions is an amazing thing to learn. Even though, predominant religion is Hindu, the tribal cultures are different. From the tribal culture evolved a unique method of worship and faith, which makes Hindu religion very fascinating. The influence of Mogul Culture (Muslim) redefined Hindu religion. Two other religions evolved out of Hinduism, the Buddhism and Jainism. The Sikh religion is an amalgamation of Hindu and Muslim religions, which also originated in India. The Christians, who are all converts from Hindus, have developed their own culture. Each caste has its own culture. Sikhs, Muslims and

Christians do not have caste system. But the caste system in Hinduism has influenced these religions also in India.

The poor people were very badly treated. I could not tolerate the mistreatment of poor and the so-called lower caste people. The rich were enjoying the life at the expense of the poor. Even now at many parts of India this continues. Government of India has many programs like reservations for admission in professional colleges and government appointments to uplift these people. It takes generations to change the customs and traditions of society in India. Civilization has yet to reach in some parts of India.

Chapter III
Childhood

I was born on May 17, 1948. My memory goes back to when I was four. The school entrance age was five. But at age four I started going to school with my sister, who was in grade two and I attended grade one. The school was a small hall with three classes. Students sit on benches and the teacher had a table, a stool and a black board to write on. We all had black slate stone with frame to write on with chalk, which get erased after. We had a book to learn the alphabets. I was officially admitted to school, when I was five in grade two. I used to get 100 points out of 100 most of the time. I used to get upset, if I got a 99.

I studied up to grade five in the same primary school operated by the Orthodox Syrian Church, which was only 1/4 mile from my house. I made my first public speech, when I was in grade two. It was a farewell party to then school headmaster, who had a big mustache. In my speech, which was written by my eldest brother, I spoke about his big mustache, which he used often to threaten the students and teachers. I did my middle school education from grade 6-8 in the private school started by our neighbor, who was an Orthodox Church priest. I was forced to attend the school, since being a new school they did not have enough students. This school was about ½ mile from my house. My high school education was in a very famous Christian school in Kottayam town about 3miles from home.

We used to walk to and from school everyday. It was fun. I was always in the top ten of the class and graduated high school with distinction. I was only fifteen, when I joined CMS College, Kottayam, one of the oldest colleges in India, started by the British missionaries in cooperation with the Syrian Christian churches. Even when I joined the college in 1963, the vice-principal was a British professor. I completed my Bachelor degree majoring in Chemistry in 1967 in first class and continued in the same college and took Master degree majoring in Analytical Chemistry at the age of 21 in 1969.

Life as a child, one among the five children, was very fascinating. There was hardly any traffic through the rough roads, except bullock carts, bicycles, pulling carts and very seldom a car or a truck. We used to play in the street most of the time. We used to make ball with coconut leaves called "OLAPPANDU" and play games like Kuzhipandu. Even though we were only three miles from town, we very seldom visited the town. We played with our neighbors, classmates and cousins, who often visited us. We could walk around freely in the farms and fields owned by our neighbors and us. We were like butterflies. People were innocent and ignorant. Almost everybody walked around bare foot. Mango, Jack fruit, cashew, coconut and banana trees supplied us with plenty of fruits.

As any other children, we used to play all day during school vacation time. One of the games was hide and seek. We had large areas to hide. Snakes were all over the place including cobra. They hide in small caves. While one of my friends was hiding behind a mud wall, he saw a cobra with its head up looking at him. The kid crying loud ran away. I used to see snakes lying around at several locations. Because of snakes, we never used to walk at night around the property. My father used to walk around with his dog and a flashlight at night and his hobby was to kill the snakes.

One day when I was in grade four, I pushed one kid when we were standing on a line and as a result several kids fell down and got hurt. The headmaster (principal) was out. The teacher in charge gave me several spanking in the back with a stick. When the headmaster came I received more spanking at the same spot. The same day my father was informed of the incident and he gave me few more at the same spot. What a day! At the age of 10, I became the president of a local chapter of a statewide children's organization sponsored by a major daily newspaper. We organized a cultural evening with music, dance and drama. It was conducted in our school grounds and temporary stage was built. We had collected some money by selling tickets to meet the expenses. The money was kept in my pocket. During the program, I slept behind the stage. When I got up, money in my pocket is gone. I got panic. My friend took me to his father, who was the president of the local government. He gave me enough money to meet the expenses. When my father found this out, I got lot of hits in the back. One time when I was with my friends to collect cashew fruits, one of my friends fell from the tree and hit a rock fifty feet below. His head was injured and taken to hospital. Luckily he survived.

Church and religion was an integral part of my childhood. We had to go to church every Sunday and also attend Sunday school. The children never worried about anything even though most of the people barely managed to make a living in my village. Industrial revolution never reached our village. I wish I could go back to those childhood days, no TV, no radio, no computer, no car, no air condition, no refrigerator, what a natural living. My father was very strict about time and what we do. We had to go to sleep early and get up early. Dinner is served only after family prayer. In the morning after we get up, we are all assigned certain work outside the house, like cleaning the yard, collecting water from the well, helping my father in gardening etc. We used to eat breakfast and dinner together as a family everyday.

When I started going to town to attend the high school, things changed. Instead of village kids, many of the town kids became my friends. School surroundings became different from a village setting to a town setting with better buildings and facilities. We had much better playgrounds and classrooms. I was still an innocent kid determined to keep up my good grades in the class. Three-mile walking to and from school was more interesting than the school, since we had a number of friends to go together. Before joining the high school, I have not seen hockey ball, which is made of cork and is very hard. I have only seen tennis balls. While coming out of the class one day, I saw a ball rolling towards me. Thinking it is a tennis ball I kicked the ball hard. Next day when I got up my right foot was all swollen and I could not walk for few days.

High school education was very good. My English teacher received the President of India award for best teacher. My school had a good reputation of being the most disciplined and providing the best education. We had to give the best performance. I remained one of the top in the class.

During summer vacation, we either used to spend our time in my house or in my mother's house. At both places all the cousins used to get together. We used to take bath in the streams or river nearby. I could not swim in the beginning and therefore, I used to stay near the shore. One of my friends offered to teach me swimming. I started swimming with his hand support. One day while we were doing this, he withdrew his hand hoping I will continue swimming. I lost my balance and went down to the bottom of the river. My friend immediately came and rescued me. My life was saved. We used to walk home from school through a railroad track to save some distance. We could cross the river either through the ferry or the railroad bridge, which is a very narrow and hollow structure. I used to prefer the ferry. One day my friends insisted that I should use the railroad bridge. There are two boxes extended from the bridge for people to stand in case the train comes. I was walking with lot of caution and about 50 feet down I heard the train coming behind me. All my friends ran to the box. I could barely walk, how can I run. My friends thought that I would be killed. I took a deep breath and ran to the box about 100 feet from me. I did not fall off the bridge. One more time my life was saved.

Girls and Boys had very little contact. In school, in the bus, in the church and every where we go, we were separated.

Therefore often we had to ignore girls. Society was cruel to us. If a girl tries to make contact with a boy, she is branded as a bad girl. Often poor girls became victims of attacks by rich men and boys. Society had no sympathy towards them. They were not prostitutes, but sometimes they were kept quite with money. They were taken advantage of. Their dreams were often shattered. The class society was dominated by the rich and the upper class, who often got away with murder.

Chapter IV
College life

My college education had three stages, a one year pre university course, a three year degree program and a two year graduate (masters degree) program. These were all full year programs from June till March. The yearly curriculum is fixed with the same weekly schedule and throughout the year the same teacher teaches the same subject. There are few mid term tests, but the final public examination which is the same for all students in all the colleges in the university. The university administers the examination and the results were published in the newspapers. Each student is given an ID number. The results were reviewed and graded by an unknown professor in another college.

Many of my classmates from high school were in my pre university class. It was a class of 80 students. English is the first language. We had the choice of taking Hindi or Malayalam as the second language. I chose Hindi and student in my class were those who have chosen Hindi and also had high grades in High School. There were eight separate pre university classes. During my degree program our major subject of study separated us. I had taken Chemistry as the major and Physics as the minor subjects. There were 36 students in the class. We had to learn English as the first language during the first two years and Hindi or Malayalam as the second language. During the language classes all women in the degree program will be in one class and all men will be in another class. During the final year of the degree program only major and subjects were taught. During the first year, there were no public examinations and at the end of the second year we had final examination for the first and second languages. At the end of the third year, all that we have been taught on the major and minor subjects during the three years were covered for the final public examination.

By the time I entered college at the age of 15 my innocence as a child was turned to wild ideas. On all major political issues, students used to rally abandoning the classes. I became one of those who provided leadership to others to enter class by class and encourage students to leave the class. To avoid violence, college authorities used to let them go. The rally was through the main streets of the town shouting slogans. Often these protest rallies against the government ended up in destruction of government properties and violence. The police used to block these rallies to avoid vandalism. One time I was in the front of one of those violent rallies and the police attacked us head on. The students got wild and started attacking the police. Police came in bigger force and started shooting. We narrowly escaped hiding behind a compound wall.

In 1964 at the age 16, I was in the first year of my three-year full time degree program. The government of India came up with a policy to abandon English as the official language and make Hindi, the only official language. Students all over southern India decided to strike with the blessing of the state governments and political parties, who also oppose the new plan. I was one of leaders to encourage students to rally. The students started attacking government of India offices and institutions like post office and destroyed signs in Hindi. Few of us decided to start a hunger strike. We built a temporary shelter in front of the college and sat there all day just drinking water. At night we used to eat by hiding some place one at a time, because police was watching us all the time. After two days, my father was informed that I am in a hunger strike. He got scared, came to college and took me home.

I liked a girl in my college. Due to restrictions in mingling with the girls, it was difficult to tell her my feelings. Finally, through a cousin of mine I gave her a love letter. Few days later I received a letter. Hoping that was the reply from the girl, all excited I opened the letter. It was from her father who was a Christian minister. He advised me to stay away from the girl. After that she would not even look at me. I met another girl while visiting my aunt in the hospital. She came to visit her mother, who was a patient in the next bed. She is from a nearby village and a student in the nearby girls high school operated by the catholic nuns. She used to stay in the school dormitory. One of her classmates was my neighbor. Through her I sent signals to her that I liked her. She agreed to meet me outside the school during lunch our, the only time she could get out. I had to rush during my lunch break in college, which is about a mile from her school, and meet her, which also is very secretly. I met her last time when she was going home for summer vacation that year. I heard that she told her parents about me and they immediately got her married to somebody at the age of 16. It was a great disappointment.

Masters program was for two full years. There were only twelve students in the class. It is always the same twelve attending a curriculum that stretches two years. We were six boys and six girls. Four girls were much older than I was. The only communication with them is during the class hours and library research. Three of us boys often used to cut classes and go for movies. Saturdays we used meet the girls in the in the library and catch up with what we have missed. Our college campus was pretty large and there were wooded areas and back roads. Lot of poor people lived in the outskirts of the college property. One day when three of us were walking through a back road, one of the girls from the poor neighborhood passed us. One of my friends grabbed her. She managed to slip away and ran for her life. We reached the dormitory where my friend was staying. In few minutes we saw a big crowd of local people coming towards our place. We hid inside the room. We heard them talking to the warden and they were saying that the person attacked the girl wore blue shirt. My friend immediately changed his shirt to a different color and escaped through the back. We came to the front asking what happened. Anyway, the crowd went back without able to identify the person.

The bus service to my village from the town was every hour. If we missed one, we had to wait an hour. Actually we could walk home by that time. Bus used to break down often and we used to walk to college about four miles. During the monsoon season, there was continuous heavy rain. Bus journey was horrible. There was three times its capacity of passengers in the bus. The four-mile ride sometimes used to take one hour, the same time as walking. Students had subsidized rates in the bus. The biggest fun was the bus journey. People from the same village, boys, girls and workers ride the morning journey together. Evening journey was mostly the students.

There was no semester system in the college. Each year certain subjects were taught throughout the year and at the end of the year there is a final examination covering the whole year. Before final examination, we used to get one-month study leave. We used to prepare for the examination. I used to study till late morning, go to sleep, wake up late, have lunch and play cards with the friends in the afternoon. The harvest season usually coincides with the study leave. During harvest time, in the middle of the paddy field there used to be a collection area and a small raised hut to take rest. At night one of us is supposed to stay in the hut to protect the harvest. One of the workers used to stay with me. There were no electric lights. Only a lantern was available. It was a quiet place to study at night. Home cooked food was delivered to us. There was also a river, where we used to take bath in the evening.

With my local friends we used to go for late movies in town. There was no bus after the movies. We had to walk four miles home. On the way home we used to enter other people's properties and plug fruits. Sometimes we used to destroy their cultivation. One day we were engaged in one of those adventures and the owner of the property was coming home late. He saw us in his property, which was a large area. He went inside and came out with a shotgun and started shooting at us. He is known to many of our parents. We started shouting loudly to him that we are sons of so and so and were just having some fun. He came to us and we all identified ourselves. The next day the whole village heard the story and it was very embarrassing.

Frog leg export to western countries was very popular. At night frog catchers was all over the low lying areas where water is collected in the paddy fields after harvest. Nobody used to eat frog legs. We decided to try it. The best time to catch the frog was at night with a flashlight. Few of us with a hired person to collect the frogs in a bag started catching frogs at night. One of our friend's fathers had an Aurvedic medicine manufacturing facility, where large wooden stove and frying pans were available. We bought the live frogs there, killed them by cutting the neck off and pulled the skin on the legs. Then we marinated them in red chili and fried in the oil. It was tasty. We continued to do this until the season for paddy cultivation started. We also used to make liquor from fruit juices. All these adventures were done without the knowledge and approval of the parents.

Since the society never permitted us to date girls or even talk to them, we were showing our frustrations at other places. But the emotions in those ages are same like other young men in any part of the world. The local social culture and traditions influence and control the emotions. I could imagine the emotions and frustrations of the girls, who had no freedom. They were not allowed to go out alone. Always somebody from the family had to accompany them. After dark, they had to stay inside the house. There are incidents where these controls were secretly broken. That was another adventure we were all engaged in.

Chapter V
Adult Life in India

Immediately after I completed the Masters Degree majoring in chemistry at the age of 21, I was appointed as a lecturer in a Christian college 18 miles away from home. Eighteen miles is too long a distance to commute, since I had to ride on three separate buses, which travels at 8 miles an hour. Therefore I stayed in a college dormitory, where some young college teachers and graduate students lived. I was the youngest teacher in the college and considered handsome. I was not ready to be an adult college teacher. My instinct was still that of a student and emotions were high. I became a popular teacher both among girls and boys. The principal (president) of the college was a Christian minister, who was also my father's classmate. He used to treat me like his son, which was very annoying at times. I was having a good time. Respect on one side and popularity on the other side. Teaching was not a problem for me since as a junior teacher, I did not have to teach Chemistry major degree students. I used to teach Chemistry minor degree students and pre degree students. I used to accompany both arts and science students during their week end sight seeing tour trips. Girls used to pass loving comments at me both in the classroom and outside. Emotions were running high and became uncontrollable at times. My roommates in the dormitory, two other young teachers used to discuss their agony too. Finally I fell in love with a young girl, which became the news of the college both among students and teachers. I managed to complete the year and decided not to continue the teaching profession. I did not marry the girl even though her father proposed to me later.

Getting a job was not that easy. I was without a job for a long time staying with my parents. I used to hang out with my local friends, playing cards, going for movies etc. I had no income, had to steal money from my fathers' pocket. After a year, I decided to live with my brother, who was in a big city called Madras, about 500 miles from home. Unemployment was so high at that time. I was over qualified for most jobs. Finally after a year my brother got me an apprenticeship in the rubber-manufacturing factory, where he worked in the export department. I also joined the rubber institute to study rubber technology. I did not enjoy the apprenticeship. Inside the factory was highly polluted. I used to come to my room with carbon all over my clothes and inside my mouth and nostrils. Once when I was returning to Madras by train after visiting my parents, I met a girl in train, who was working as a nurse in a medical college 150 miles from Madras. We became friends. I visited her several times. During that time US government was giving immigrant visa to nurses, doctors and other professionals. She also applied for a visa and through sponsorship by her classmate already an immigrant in USA she obtained a visa.

We decided to get married before she leaves for USA. With great difficulty we convinced our parents and with hesitation they agreed for our wedding on May 28, 1973. My wife, Somini left for USA in June 1973 and I joined her in December 1973.

My adult life in India was interesting mainly because of I had lot of friends. For one year as a teacher I mingled with the students and teachers as well. Weekend I spent time with my classmates and local friends. There was no direct contact with women. We were supposed not to have sex before marriage. This made it impossible to have a relationship with a woman. Since it was a normal social norm, everybody accepted it the way it was. This may have been one of the reasons why people got married early in life, women at the age of 16-20 and men at the age of 21-25. I got married at the age of 25.

Once you become an adult earning member of the family, it is your responsibility to support the family. If there are children younger than you, it is your responsibility to help them until they become adult earning members of the family. Therefore, nobody used to spend money for unnecessary expenses. Life was tough except for a very few rich people. The main entertainment was playing cards, going for movies and hanging out with other men. There was no bar to hang out and even to hang out in a restaurant on a regular base was not affordable. Therefore we used to gather at the YMCA or in the street corners. The biggest fun was looking at girls passing by and making comments. In fact if the father, husband or brother accompanied the women, we were afraid to even look. But if a woman was alone in the bus or in the crowd, they were often attacked. If we were in USA, we would have all been arrested for sexual molestation. In fact women used to keep quite or move away, when those things happened. If they openly complain, they would have ended up as bad girls.

Chapter VI
Life in USA

My married life actually began in USA, since my wife left few days after the wedding. By the time I arrived at USA, my wife was already working as nurse in a hospital in Newark, New Jersey. We moved into an apartment in Broadway. My wife used to take bus to downtown Newark and walk to the hospital. She worked the evening shift till midnight. I used to meet her in front of the hospital after work and we used to come home together. Everything seemed to be normal at that time. We could not afford any luxuries. We did not have a TV or car. We used to go to her friend's house to watch TV. We bought some used furniture. The materialism did not hit us yet. After few months we bought a Pontiac, Ventura. A friend of ours cosigned the loan.

My cousin helped me get a job as chemist in the City of Newark, water supply and I started on April 29, 1974. I am still working for Newark water supply. I joined Stevens Institute of Technology, Hoboken, New Jersey and completed my Masters degree program in Environmental Engineering in 1980. I was promoted as Water Quality Supervisor and in 1978, I became the Superintendent of Water treatment. Later I was promoted to Principal Environmental Specialist, then to Supervising Environmental Specialist and in 1989 became the Supervising Engineer. In 1998 I was assigned as the

Manager of the water treatment plant. My wife always worked as a staff nurse.

As young couple, our life started in America and blossomed into a full family. In the beginning we had only few friends of our age group, all of them recent immigrants from India. All of our friends were either our classmates or people from our state in India, Kerala. We slowly got accustomed to the culture and surroundings. Many things we saw were surprising to us especially men and women kissing in the open, cuddling together in the bus or even holding hand and walking together. In India women used to walk few feet behind men. I was thinking of the things I might have missed as a young man. When I first saw the sign YMWCA in Newark, I could not believe it. In India women were not allowed in YMCA and men were not allowed in YWCA. What a contrast it was? Even if you are married, you were not allowed to kiss in the open in India. Your lovemaking had to be secret mainly in the bedroom. Like all our friends from India, we had the obligation to help and support our families in India, whose standard of living was very poor compared to USA. Therefore we did not spend money on luxuries, saved to send to our parents.

The great cultural shock we encountered was unbelievable. Moving from an underdeveloped country of age old traditions influenced by the Hindu religion, where caste system and discrimination of the poor were the way of life to a well developed country, dominated by Christian and western culture resulted in a great astonishment. I grew up in a village with poor infrastructure and poor means of life. Social pressure influenced my behavior and determined whom I associate with. The state of Kerala, where I grew up had good educational institutions because of Christian influence. We learned English as a second language in the school and the medium of instruction in the college was English. We had no knowledge of the western culture. Even now, my culture is very much rooted in India, where I lived till the age of 25. We are leading a double life. Outside we are Americans and inside we are Indians.

In the year 1974, the gasoline shortage due to gulf war and the resignation of the American President Nixon were shocking news to us. I remember lining up in front of the gasoline station to get limited amount of gas. When President Nixon resigned, the transition to President Ford was smooth. The two-year term of President Ford and the one term of Jimmy Carter were not good economic times for USA. The American hostage situation in Iran in 1979 ruined the pride of America. The two-term era of President Reagan brought back pride and patriotism and the economy also was improved. The four-year term of President Bush was dominated by the Iraq war, the desert storm. President Bush failed to maintain economic progress, which resulted in the election of President

Clinton. The two terms President Clinton created an atmosphere of economic well being to Americans and an era of peace. Clinton's last six years were perhaps the best economic times in the history of USA. President George W. Bush elected amidst controversy in Florida state did not have a good start. The economic recession began. September 11, 2001 terrorist attack on the World Trade Center twin buildings in New York City and Pentagon Building in Virginia shocked the whole World. This was a barbaric attack on America killing thousands and a threat to the free World. President Bush responded with courage and determination. There were lot of developments in other parts of the World. Everything had an influence on me. My outlook to life was molded by the political, religious and racial events in USA as well as around the World. I am an optimist and believe in fate. No force in the World can stop an event from happening. Life is unpredictable.

My first child, a girl, Simmy was born on November 12, 1974 and the second child, a boy, Kevin was born on November 28,1978. Both grew up in the new age of technological advancement and scientific revolution. Since the early seventies, scientific and technological advances were tremendous. When I first came to USA, there were no fax, car phone or cell phone. There was no personal computer with user friendly programs. Texas instruments produced a scientific calculator priced at $400 to $500. Now information technology has been revolutionized and everybody at home enjoys the fruits through Internet, DVD, etc. Things that were not in the imagination of our generation have become realities. Our children grew up as US citizens with an Indian identity. In schools they were often mistaken as foreigners. Their fellow students subjected my children to discrimination. It was hard for them to understand the reason for the misbehavior by the fellow students. At times even the teachers treated them like children of foreigners, who do not speak English. The color prejudice combined with ignorance was evident in the behavior our neighbors and colleagues at work. As years went by everybody started accepting each other. The number of Indian immigrants increased. Our children grew to become adults.

I started getting involved in community activities. Indian organizations were formed every where. I was involved in forming Kerala Association, Indian Organization and Asian American Political Coalition. I also got involved in political activities. Christian churches from Kerala, India started congregations and parishes. Indian community became visible and I became one of the known leaders of the Indian American community. Our social friends were mainly Malayalees, the people from the state of Kerala, India. As they grew up, our children had mostly friends of Indian origin. America, the melting pot of all cultures, is a fascinating country. Since I grew up in a very traditional underdeveloped country, I could appreciate the greatness of America. My children cannot comprehend this and so also many Americans.

Chapter VII
Life through generations

The narrative story of my life probably portrays same as that of any other immigrant from India. But, I see it differently. When I grew up, I never realized that there was a life beyond what I saw. Go to school, get a degree, find a good career, get married, have a family, lead a good life and bring up a new generation. I never thought of going to USA and building a family. Life in India did not give me much of a hope. It was mostly one day at a time and static. My transformation to a rich western country changed my outlook. Life suddenly became dynamic. I saw progress everywhere. Living conditions of the poor in USA is better than the living conditions of the so-called middle class in India. A boy who grew up in a village under primitive conditions without enjoying the luxuries of life becomes an independent adult with a good career living in luxury.

Living through generations in an underdeveloped country is no way comparable to living in a wealthy western country. There are the good sides and bad sides. Often when I visit India, I compare the life in both countries. Progress in India is slow, while the pace of progress is very fast in USA. Scientific and technological progress reaches the common man, while in India it is experienced by a small percentage of the population. My parent's dream has become realities for my generation, my dreams have become realities for my children and their dreams will become realities for my grand children. Each generation has a unique experience. As one generation fades away, a new generation blossoms. A person could experience living through three or four generations. Each generation lives through a different experience and culture. History tries to link generations. A new generation is fortunate to hear about the experiences and events of the past generations. The older generation never finds out the experiences of the new generation. Unless one lives through and experiences it, it either remains a story or a dream.

The culture of a generation is influenced by the history, religion, political events, scientific and technological developments, contemporary arts, educational system, economic conditions, trade, communication systems, region of the world and the time period. The contemporary culture and events influence a person. I was influenced by several cultures. My parents grew up in a small kingdom in the southwestern corner of India, which later joined Independent India. My parents were descendants of generations of Christians from A.D 52, when St. Thomas one of the Disciples of Christ supposed to have visited our part of India and converted few families to Christianity. Three religions flourished in our area, Hindu,

Muslim and Christian. I was born and bought up in free India. My children are born citizens of USA. I spent most of my adult life in USA. As I lived through different times, my life style changed, my thought process expanded and my personality developed. My culture went through series of changes.

When a person live in an age and place where there is no scope for higher dreams and aspirations, it is like a frog living alone at the bottom of a deep well. It has never seen the outer world and all it knows is the wall around. It cannot even climb up to see anything. This was my experience when I grew up in an underdeveloped country surrounded by poor people. Since, my parents were literate, I at least had the opportunity to read newspapers and books. But still most of the things were beyond my imagination. I believed everything my parents, teachers, friends and neighbors told me. They influenced me very much. I was very happy, since I did not have knowledge about a better life, like the frog in the well. My horizon was very limited. Once in high school and college, my knowledge expanded. Industrialization of India provided new opportunities and experience. New influences started changing my personality. My innocence started fading away. I started questioning some of the social customs and traditions.

Living through a generation questioning and challenging the social and cultural traditions equipped me with higher goals. I wanted to change the world, change the way people behave, act and think. I wanted to develop a distinct personality. I was restricted in my actions because of my limited resources. The new thinking culture influenced lot of my contemporaries. In fact a new political thought emerged and young people became actively involved in political process. When the rest of India was struggling to improve literacy among its citizens, the people in our state were getting basic education. Education and educated people around me influenced in the development of my culture.

I experienced my first cultural shock when I moved to live in a big cosmopolitan city in another state in India at the age of 22. In India the language, culture and social customs and traditions are unique in different parts. I saw people of different culture and tradition speaking different language and being a cosmopolitan city, people from all over India live there. I was influenced by Kerala culture of Malayalam speaking people. In the big city, it was mostly Tamil speaking people with different culture. I was living with my brother in a small one-bed room apartment; much different from the spacious house I grew up surrounded by open spaces and farms. Wandering through the big city looking for a job I experienced many things. I used to visit the library at the American consulate. I developed friendship with lot of Malayalees, who are a major population in Madras. There were lot of people from my college also.

While unemployed, I read many books. I read Ramayana, the Hindu epic and teachings of Swami Vivekananda, the great Hindu philosopher who lived in the nineteenth century and visited USA. My thought became more philosophical. My outlook to life was changed. I became agitated because of my inability to find a job. I wanted to get out of India. I experienced hopelessness and despair like most of the educated unemployed people in India. This resulted in an exodus of educated people from India to other countries in pursuit of finding a job. India at that time called it a brain drain. This brain drain in the nineteen seventies later turned out to be helpful to India.

The generation gap was fast widening. My grand parents lived in a small kingdom, which became part of India after independence from the British rule. India consisted of many kingdoms. British combined it into one area for the easy administration. The British made it possible for people to travel from one Kingdom to other. They connected India by constructing a large railway system. Living in a small kingdom and living in a large country with democratically elected government were altogether different experiences for my parents. I lived in free India. The political changes, the economic growth, the industrialization, the scientific development, advances in communication and the new educational system that occurred during the period of three generations widened the generation gap. My migration to USA and my children growing up during the time of triumphant advancements in science and technology further widened the gap between my parents and me and my children and me.

My children's generation all over the world is exposed to many things because of the development of Internet and easy availability of information. Information and communication is the key to human progress. The new 21st century generation will loose respect for history. They are a fast moving generation. They are always looking ahead and have no time to look back. Their values have changed. They cannot comprehend a life without cell phones and Internet. Instant availability of information on all world events makes the world smaller.

The world is changed. But the human conflicts continue. None of these advances including revolutionized changes in communication and information technology has any impact on human reactions and basic human instincts. What we really see is change in outside appearances and actions. Inside human being is still struggling to find the ultimate goal of life.

Chapter VIII
Ultimate Goal of Life

What is the ultimate goal of life? What is the meaning of life? Do I lead a proper life? What did I gain from my life experiences? What is my contribution to the next generation? How do we explain the sudden breakthrough in science and technology? What makes me a better person? Do we have control over the events in life? Is there a life after death? So many questions come through our mind. Most of the events in our life were not predicted. When I look back I see a life full of events and incidents, but with no real meaning. Days, nights, weeks, months and years go by. Life and death, war and conflicts, celebrations and joyous occasions, accidents and mishaps, scientific inventions and technological advancements; nothing seems to have any real meaning. Time is passing in such a fast pace that I seem to be standing alone and life is passing me, rather than I am passing the life. One day I will disappear and those who saw me standing alone in the path of life will wonder for a moment what would have happened to me. Soon they will forget me. Generation by generation human beings disappear from this world. Everybody passes through this world only once. Nobody, those who live in the dark corners of the world, those who participate in the advances of science and technology, the rich, the poor, the wicked, the nice, the murderer, the philanthropist, the monarch, the autocrat, the president, the prime minister, the beautiful, the ugly, the powerful, and the powerless, can escape death. Death is inevitable. Who lived a good or bad life? Who made contributions to the world? Who destroyed humanity? Who helped humanity? The answers do not matter.

I searched through history. I looked through my life. I looked at others. I looked at my parents. I looked at my wife and children. I looked at my friends and colleagues. I looked at my religious and political leaders. Nobody seems to worry about the ultimate goal of life. I looked at religion for an answer. Religion speaks about faith, which results in an eternal life after death in a place of love and peace. If we cannot have love and peace in this world, how can we expect it in another world? If the goal of life is to achieve a life after death, one must thrive for it by following a perfect life. That means the life in this world will be same as the life after death. Therefore death is the end of life. I cannot imagine a life after death. What you see and experience in this world is life. Therefore one must be prepared to face life as it comes to you. The mind is programmed in such a way that one could face good times, bad times, poverty, wealth, death, destruction, peace, celebration, sorrow, love and hatred. Because of the ups and downs in life, one does not have time to think about the ultimate goal of life. A handful of religious leaders, philosophers and thinkers tried to define the ultimate goal of life. They have not succeeded.

Animals and birds do not have an ultimate goal. They are part of ecology. Human beings are also part of ecology. If that is the case why should they have an ultimate goal? Be part of ecology and disappear. How come human beings can think, communicate and act intelligently? If the law of evolution is true, how come only human beings can do all these? How come frogs and monkeys cannot talk? What is the purpose and function of universe? Why human beings are only on earth? What happens if the earth and universe disappear? When is the end of the world? Where is this eternal world? How does human beings travel to the eternal world after death? There are more and more questions we cannot answer. The eternal world has to be somewhere in the world. What we see is the real world. The world will be here forever and therefore this is the eternal world. One experiences the result of one's actions in this world.

Why there are people of different color and shape? Why do people speak different languages? Why people of one race think they are better than another race? Why there are many religions? What is the purpose of religion? Why people fight in the name of religion? How come civilization did not reach all parts of the world at the same time? Again we have questions without answers. If we can find answers to many of these questions, it becomes easier to determine the ultimate goal of life. Religion is personal and each person's religious experience is unique. Religion speaks about a way of life to reach the eternal world after death. Each religion has a separate definition of God, purpose of life and path to eternity. Can we be blind believers and lead a normal life? Does religion provide a purpose for life other than looking forward for eternal life after death? Can we depend on the religion for our salvation? If the eternal world is here on earth, why do we have to wait for it? We can start experiencing the eternal world right from the beginning of life in the real world. In other words we must celebrate our life while we are alive. Do not wait for death to celebrate life. Like the civil law enforcement by the government, religion enforces the law of God, which are man-made. If the religious laws are not followed, the punishment is the denial of eternal world, which is supposed to be decided by God, not by man. In other words, man creates the religion in the name of God. The question is whether you need religious laws in this world. If everybody understands the goal of life, religion becomes irrelevant. Therefore people follow religion to find a purpose for life.

Why each generation faces different situations and has different experience? Human pursuit for progress results in different experiences for each generation. Human progress cannot be used to measure human behavior. Conflicts between nations, religious followers and races still continue. If the purpose of life is revealed to everybody, many of these human conflicts will not occur.

The ultimate goal of life is actually defined by each individual. If one can be reminded about the inevitable death on every day, the meaning of life will be explored. If one can believe that the only life that can be experienced is the one on this earth, then a goal can be set. Some people choose to be thieves and murderers, some people choose to be religious and political leaders, some people choose to be selfish and greedy and some people choose to promote love and peace. Some people change their attitude towards life after some bad experiences. Based on the location of birth, economic conditions, educational opportunities and political environment, each person has unique experiences and opportunities in this world. There are mishaps and misfortunes in life. Some experience good times and good fortunes.

Regardless of the experiences and opportunities, one must celebrate life in full extent. While celebrating life one must not hurt the feelings of others, rather provide opportunities to others also to celebrate their life. This must be the goal of life. There is only one life to live and live it right. We must make the world a better place to live by our deeds.

Andreos

About the Author

Andrew Pappachen is a resident in the State of New Jersey, USA. He was born in India in the year 1948. He migrated to USA at the age of twenty-five. Andrew completed his master's degree majoring in chemistry in India. He took a master's degree in environmental engineering from Stevens Institute of Technology, New Jersey. The City of Newark, New Jersey, has employed him since 1974. He is married and they have two grown up children.

Andrew has been very active in community activities for the past twenty-five years. He has been the president of various Indian American, Asian and other community and cultural organizations. He has received several awards in recognition for his contributions to the community.

Andrew has a very unique perspective of life. He is an optimist. He strongly believes that there is no life after death. Having born in India, a poor underdeveloped country, he received the best opportunity for education. He also took advantage of the opportunities in the United States and was successful in developing a career. He faces life one day at a time. He never complains about life. He knows that the events of life are often unpredictable.

Andrew wants to fulfill his life by serving humanity more. But he is restricted because of his family obligations and limited financial resources. Andrew believes that if each person is willing to make some positive contribution to the humanity, life in this world will become enjoyable to all. Andrew says, "There is only one life to live and live it right".